WRITERS COLLECTIVE

Poems by 19 Writers
Portland, Oregon
1998

Carl Adamshick
Kelly Lenox Allan
Sophie Crawford
Michele Glazer
Trudy Godat
Melanie Green
Michael Griggs
Eric Hull
Christy Hurt
Arthur Irwin
Ursula Irwin
Tracy Klein
Katharine Miller
Sabine Miller
Mary Misel
Quigley Provost-Landrum
Tom Richards
Richard Sanders
Patricia Staton Thomas

Michele Glazer, Editor

QUIET LION PRESS
Portland, Oregon

Writers Collective ©1998 Writers Collective

Cover Photographs: Trudy Godat

This book may not be reproduced in whole or in part without the express written consent of the publisher and/or the individual writers with whom the copyrights remain, with the exception of short excerpts included in critical articles or reviews. All other rights reserved.

Writers Collective wishes to thank the following people for their generosity, patience and guidance in bringing this anthology into print: Brian Christopher of Quiet Lion Press, Dan at Dan Fast Printing, Mike Tracker at Rose City Bindery, Kandace Grey Thorns of Ariel Productions, Melissa Tracker, Kelly Allan and Melanie Green.

ISBN 1-882550-33-1

Printed in USA

QUIET LION PRESS
7215 S.W. LaView Drive
Portland, Oregon 97219
(503) 771-1907

Contents

Katharine Miller
    Boat / 7
    Badlands / 8
    Orbit / 9
    My Friend's Son, At Three / 10
    Balinese Woman / 11
    Ceremony / 12

Quigley Provost-Landrum
    Transubstantiation/ 13
    Pilgrim's Progress / 15
    The Wishing/ 16
    Meditation On a Mother I Do Not Know / 17
    Reading / 18
    Declaration Of Love In The New York City Port Authority
        Bus Terminal OR The Continuance Of The Unreal / 19

Melanie Green
    Even When It Rains / 20

Richard Sanders
    Postscript To Desire / 21
    Short Power Failure / 22
    Untitled /23
    Waiting For Spring / 24

Sophie Crawford
    According To My Fortune Cookie It Is Better To Have
        A Hen Tomorrow Than An Egg Today / 25
    Wish / 26
    Natural Lives / 27
    Memory Game / 28
    Apocalyptic / 29
    Poem For J. Sands / 30

Tracy Klein
    Moonwalk 1969 / 31
    Pneumonia Poem / 32
    Nursing Internship, LA County, 1990 / 33
    Another LA Poem / 34
    Trip To Albuquerque / 35
    Eel / 36

Christy Hurt
    On A Painting At The Children's Psychiatric Facility / 37
    On The Sandy River, I Find In Wood, Thoughts Of A
        Bitter Sister / 38
    My Sister's Photo . . . Dated 1973 . . . She's Twenty Years Old
        And Very Pretty / 40

Sabine Miller
    Headache Rock / 42
Ursula Irwin
    Brush Strokes / 43
    Benediction / 44
Trudy Godat
    Treed / 46
    Untitled / 47
    Enclosing The Circle / 48
    Scattered Out / 49
Carl Adamshick
    Sense / 50
    Lizbeth / 51
    Worship / 53
    —Customs Of Grace / 54
Michele Glazer
    Letter / 55
    All That In The Voice I Have Adopted For This Lie / 57
    Science / 58
Tom Richards
    Lessons Of A Blacksmith / 59
    With Her Husband . . . / 61
    Five A.M. In The Jericho Beach Hostel / 63
Arthur Irwin
    Seagulls / 64
Kelly Lenox Allan
    Memories Like This / 65
    Dowsing /66
    A Driver. A Heart Attack. / 67
    This Season / 68
Eric Hull
    Untitled/ 69
    Untitled/ 70
    The Patch / 71
Mary Misel
    Grinding / 73
Michael Griggs
    Letter To A Cruel Mother / 74
Patricia Staton Thomas
    Hex, Unhex / 75
    Father's Day At Snapp's Cottages / 77
    Pommes De Terre / 78
    Maladies Of The Heart, Vol. 7 / 79
    Love Poem / 81

The Writers Collective / 82

Katharine Miller

BOAT

All color is metal
and my shoulders are cold

as I skim
the bluish surface off the water
to the black under.
The grasses shudder on the shore.

Through the night water,
I thrust forward,
enduring the wind on my throat.

My lungs resemble
a pair of blue feathered breasts.
Breath comes awkwardly,
like flight to a largelimbed heron.

The curve of my body
does not betray
my rigidity, arms locked
at my sides, I am steadfast.

Looking up, I envy the moon,
so coveted by the night sky.
I envy its stillness
and its ability to be
such a small white bird.

BADLANDS

The only shadows
are the hulks of grazing bison.

The rest is grass,
bristling,
except where it is flattened
by some sleek body.

Bustled by wind
huge animals shift
from foot to foot, stomping.
The wind conduces a kind of swallowing.

The meadow crackles with insects.

ORBIT

For three nights now
I've noticed the moon
in its pregnancy.
(tonight it's a lopsided egg.)

Noticing reminds me
of our night in the forest.
While we sectioned the oranges
la luna was rising.

Still I taste the rust
from those fruits on my fingers.
So much of what we share
tastes like skin.

MY FRIEND'S SON, AT THREE

I.
Sitting on the deck by the pool,
naked boy
picks up insects, places them,
neat like seeds
in a row, on his erect penis.

II.
The chart is for children,
animal shapes in rows, bigger to smaller.
Another eye test.
Asked what he sees,
Lars answers solemnly,
nothing living nor dead.

III.
He is matter-of-fact about it. Ice cream
dripping from the corner of his mouth
forms a perfect right angle with the line of his lips.
This is his first ice cream soda.
He sits straight in the red sparkle booth,
clenches his spoon.

IV.
At four, he falls in love with a Russian girl.
On his back under a tree,
his mother finds him, beckons, come on, it's time to go.
No longer three, he protests the interruption.
Don't disturb me while I'm lying here with my heart.

BALINESE WOMAN

Her gnarled feet
carve a path
down the
steep
hillside.
Narrow, brown woman
balancing
a crude basket.
Her long back,
the quiet
groove of her hips.
Down
the slope of the
terraced ricefield,
she walks.
Clay breasted,
she carries her laundry
to the river.
She will wash the clothes
among the stones.
She will pour soap powder
into the river.
She will lay the
soaked clothes
in the basket.
Her face will
crease
when she lifts it.
Silent,
she will stand
before the climb.
Basket on her head,
she will know the
weight
of it.

CEREMONY

This is our last drink in New York,
peach blossom tea.
I will remember this as Spring Street.

The teahouse,
from the chill of the darkening street,
an illuminated place.

Tea, the color of candlelight,
chimes
in white china cups.

Here, only the teapot with its
flawed spout
leaks a cooled puddle onto the table

and reminds us
to be tired.

Quigley Provost-Landrum

TRANSUBSTANTIATION

On the seventh day He rested.
We've barely been able to rouse Him since.
It wasn't naiveté but faith.
Not believing but knowing her own breath
could stop, catch, hold itself squeezing
back into the lungs, into the heart.

Sweeping the fog at the edge
of the crucifix she could hear
the Greeks at the window cackle
at the price of life. God didn't
look at him hard enough. Hardly
enough. The days they had played together

swelled like the Gulf of Mexico.
He hummed "Skylark," trembling yellow,
gold, brown. Like fall. *I wish you were
my brother.* His almond lips
reminded her of glass. Cracked,
broken, drawing blood. Exchanging

blood for blood, she could see
the current running
beneath the high yellow skin of his arms.
Arms like hers. In her dream
the night before, her cat came to her
its wound open deep in its chocolate fur.

Would he know what her question was?
Where the host goes once you've touched
your tongue to the unleaven?
You must hold your breath to receive it.
You must close your eyes. Witness
God's eyes in your sleepless sleep.

Days later they bathed his feet
with chrism. Folded him beneath
a dead crape myrtle near the fence.

No one was quiet. There was a keening.
There was a clapping of hands.
There was weakness in the fingers that move to hold.

God doesn't answer when you cry.
only in the quiet deep holding
of breath between weeping and sleep.

PILGRIM'S PROGRESS

I rode with them in the car from Houston
to Lafayette in withering August heat.
(I don't remember August,
only the watermelon I broke
trying to show off my nine-year-old strength).
Driving with my mother and my aunts,
my cousin the nun leading the recitation
of the rosary along the way.

We were on our way to see the image
of Christ on some old woman's screen door.
And I don't remember much. Only driving
for a long time and worrying
if someone might cut my hair and anoint
my head with oil or make me spit

into a frog's mouth again as a cure
for my asthma. When we arrived,
there must have been a hundred people there
already a hundred people making the red dust
rise from their sandals up to their ankles

and knees. Trampling the purple jew
that struggled in the parched yard, they sang
Holy God We Praise Thy Name. I couldn't see.
All that dust and distance and a broken watermelon.
I heard people around me say they could see Him.
That He moved and wept in the screen
I only saw Him in my mother's gloved hand
clutching the scapular. I only saw Him
in the choking, dust-laden jew.

THE WISHING

Already you have your heart set on me.

Twelve years it seems have taught you nothing.
I am incapable of normal work. So bored already
I hurt behind my eyes. Menus are what I cultivate.
Risotto with savoy and roast chicken with too much
garlic. You see how useless I am.

The daughter, she passed again this morning.
Sloping forehead fixed at the thought in front of her.
The molded plastic doll with one eye, secure
in its sling bound to her chest, looking for a moment
like a real baby. But what would she be doing
with a real baby? The small arm sticks out stiffly.
The make-believe diaper bag, I could see, was empty.
The damage lingers here between us.

I have developed, after years of sleeping with you,
the habit of morning thirst. As if waking in a desert.
It's a secret what I do when you sleep. I rock myself
and do not need your permission. Your forgiveness.
Your hands. I am my own absolution.

You see I have nothing to offer you. Only my prayers
for more poems and waiting for the dark to break.
I am most afraid when the dark removes itself
from the corners of the house.
I want to live with the untrimmed rose bushes.
With the puddle of mosquitoes bleeding sunset
into night.

MEDITATION ON A MOTHER I DO NOT KNOW

How will I know who you are? I've only ever glimpsed
you in my mind's eye. I could press the flashlight
against my hand, illuminating the blood beneath
the skin surrounding bone. You might find me.
Brush the air for webs connecting us. Tap my rings
against your mirror. They pressed too hard
with the forceps at the delivery. You can read
my struggle in the lumps left there. I pushed
my knees into the air and slapped at the anger
in the long bones of my thighs looking for you. Do you
press your shoulder blades together, pale and sweating,
recalling the shock in my eyes? Yesterday,
in my garden, I shook the pupae suspended
from the trees. Squatting beneath God I sowed
your bruised and callused skin into the earth
with the crocuses. Watched the compost breathe
beneath my nails. I want you to listen
for my breathing in this earth. Tonight I will thread
my needle of bone with my own hair. Embroider
what I remember onto that last remaining linen napkin.
I will praise you with the work of my body,
the work of my hands.

READING

My father saws two-by-fours.
Measures, reads the level bounding

into the moon's eye. Nails pieces
until, without flourish, they

outwit hurricanes. He tracks
doe and buck through heavy snows.

Skins, guts, watches the water
wash the blood from his cracked skin.

Sitting in a green boat reading
his line, setting his net for gar,

he laughs at the time he courted
my mother by pretending

he played the guitar. He makes
a courtbouillon to make your mouth

a glad witness to the day.
He is composed of red clay

and air. He reads the landscapes
by feel. He cannot read this.

DECLARATION OF LOVE IN THE NEW YORK CITY PORT AUTHORITY BUS TERMINAL
OR
THE CONTINUANCE OF THE UNREAL

After I propose,
marriage rings ominously.
You leave. Winter comes.

Melanie Green

EVEN WHEN IT RAINS

Today, cutting daffodils
from the untended garden
next to the garage
grasping wet stems in my hand,
how easily they were bent
or crushed.

Sizing long stems to the height
of my joy
the trumpeting yellow
I had to gather in
to be mine.

Choosing a vase, I pick
the sky-grey
pitcher speckled with brown,
the broken
handle glued back on.

From the untended garden
inside me the yellow
whispers:

> *are you remembering*
> *what you love?*

Richard Sanders

POSTSCRIPT TO DESIRE
(We are not some journey our children take to die)

I think of the dead body of my son
and my mind looks out dirty windows
heavy rains cannot clean.

I think of that worn mattress in his room
and that final note without my name on it.

My keyboard fills with cloudy lands so dark
they weary the fiercest wind
and children will not play there.

I am almost 20 years from Aaron's death.
Too many years without new memories
and I no longer believe time is chronology.

SHORT POWER FAILURE

Suddenly the heat is primitive.
Dusk threatens civilization.
The tv picture implodes;
Dan Rather becomes an infinite point of light.
Clocks run counter to our lives:
Time disjoints us like a train
Moving slowly forward
outside our stationary window,
propelling us backwards
against all will of senses.
The sky bellies low, the valley seems
to raise hips in roaring copulation,
and then comes, an explosion
of plummeting temperature,
howling thunder, lightning and rain;
suddenly the rain slows to a gentle sweat,
the house of night flickers on,
the television catches light, blooms full
on shattered children in Sarajevo,
and all is right with the world again.

UNTITLED

In this cell of my singing
I am a distant song
confined in an age of memory
like the loneliness of an envelope
with only a bill enclosed
forwarded
from a woman who loved me once

WAITING FOR SPRING

Hope has such a lovely way of diddling us
as we become its echoes.

Sophie Crawford

ACCORDING TO MY FORTUNE COOKIE IT IS BETTER TO HAVE A HEN TOMORROW THAN AN EGG TODAY

I've already decided to live forever.
Nobody's going to crack this egg and poach it.

No hen will ever drop an egg
as smooth as this one.

I was the one who found the real
egg dyed robin's blue,

hidden among bright impostors
at the Sunday School Easter hunt.

I could smell the sulfur of the kingdom on my hands.
I was never going to die

unlike the hen clucking feebly
in the slow-cooked air of the brooder house.

I won't be groomed to feed anyone.
I'll nest in purple velvet

on a window sill, let light
penetrate me

like the girl god fucked.
I'll be rubbed for luck.

I'll fly through the afternoon
between the tingling grasps of children

who know I am as raw
as ice. I'll be pocketed,

etched with impossible gardens.
My landscape will never look the same twice.

WISH

As children we wanted to be lost.
To sleep all night
in the forest.

We knew the difference—woods
flickered, sky, leaves,
hotbed of ferns, poison oak.

The winking trail of marbles
we dropped for those who would not come looking
led only to itself.

Our hair grew to our knees.
We learned to eat fire-
blackened flesh; blackberries

so rare in that density
we devoured a thicket like a house of candy.
Sometimes between distant trunks

we caught sight of her
lugging water from the stream,
or kindling, an old woman

obsessed with peppermint, gingerbread.
She gave us a bed in her cupboard.
We pretended to be asleep

when she nibbled our shoulders.
Like grandchildren we followed her
to the cut glass dish

full of lemon drops
when she called us her sweets.
We pushed her into the oven

because she was afraid
the fire might not wrap her in its arms,
she might outlive us.

NATURAL LIVES

Nancy'd strike a match,
shred shoe boxes,
orange flannel pajamas—
that bitch of a landlady
poked a hole up
the scut-clogged chimney, about time,
Nancy'd thrust her tits,
neck into the fire
glow.

In August afternoons she'd lie the length
of the nubby blue-green sofa,
tendrils of auburn hair striating
her neck, the blue veins rippling
her legs, thighs like twin salamanders
splayed in the egg-yolk light, writing
as if she could pull
and suck on words with her mother's tongue.

Writing, that seismic scratch—
Nancy shrieked for me at 5 a.m.
when our building jumped and swaggered.
Cassette tapes in their plastic suitcases
toppled, the apartment
rocking, crying my name.
Out of bed I was naked,
couldn't decide about my bathrobe
as the walls, the floor ceased.
Nancy curled in her spumoni quilt,
eyes telescoped, waiting to ride one more tremor.

MEMORY GAME

Through my morning window
I watch a Dalmatian frisk
in wet uncut grass, the blossoming
lilac where he rubs, remember little
of the long night.
I pretended sweetness, neon
light danced between leaves, days
of chattering. The man with me:
a flash of teeth, signs
winking off his glasses between
black trunks of maples. The man with me:
a shouldering of black
leather, an impatient spreading of palms,
a closeness, a gap between words.
Old, the dog's owner gulps honey with tea
—how orange the moon
was when she met her husband, how fat.
I threw up everything, in love. At night
I brush close to the forgotten,
its smoke-drinking hide, its breath
a room inside the body.
I see that the man was perfect:
black hair roughing white skin, eyes
the mauve of lilacs, unlimited
touches of the hand. *Unlimited
how I believed myself his opposite.*

APOCALYPTIC

Although I have learned enough of the language
of maps, I may not find my way home, the night
unlit, the rash of every surface
pricking. I drag my body through tight
muscles, the base of my throat swollen
like the furry gullet of a gym sock,
my chronic bark encouraged by pollen
sifting quiet as owls through the shocks
of pines. I should sit up to my chin
in water burning like the tropic of Capricorn—
nurse my disease stubbornly, flame-eyed, a thin
beard of orange syrup trickling, an object of scorn.
I keep thinking I will cough up blood soon.
My mouth will mirror the infected moon.

POEM FOR J. SANDS

He looks hungry
for it, spring grass
or smokable,
lusting for green.
If his lamb-fleece
hair were golden
he'd be Jesus
but he's speechless
with gratitude,
brings the doctor
flowers, African
violets and
pink cyclamen
for letting him know
he waited too
long, should have had
that lump measured
at twenty-three.
Needing to count
no more years, he
smiles weakly
from a labyrinth
of tie-dye, his
name reminds me
of "Come Unto
These Yellow Sands."
I think he longs
for sleep, the sound
of an ocean
he cannot see.

Tracy Klein

MOONWALK 1969

I'm in the swimming pool
smelling of rubber and chlorine.
I've learned to keep my eyes open
playing a favorite game:
sinking to the bottom, lungs puffed
with intention, thumbing up silver
car keys as a risky challenge.
Alone, I couldn't be more happy at my fortune:
no one wants to play with me.
In the July air (month of my birthday)
buffed cars slumber in their numbered spaces.
Every identical living room has its tinkling chandelier
turned off, occupants squinting to keep cool.
They are like bored animals, waiting at the food bowl.
Televisions on, they hope to become a historic moment.
Around my head, my favorite moon white rubber cap
with sparkling starfish keeps my hair from coming loose,
from catching in knots which would make my father angry.
He is up there, with the rest of them.
Above me, each apartment sports its own light
green as the pool, each television casts its jerking picture
across the landscape. Bulky chairs grow undershirted Dads,
Moms lurk behind the window pouring jello salad on a plate.
The jello will be cool, not fussy.
I am water-walking, without wings to hold me up.
The men on television in their heavy suits
lumber tentatively, stepping out for their first dip
in the white, lustrous, unknown
surface of the moon.

PNEUMONIA POEM

Age ate down his fortune
like a piece of cheese and he
bit hard to live with what he'd made:
a bed with a small view of the apple
tree, a handkerchief,
a glass of water, a picture frame
with colored Xerox to represent
the hearty halos of his Mother and Dad.
He loved them for the fact that,
as a kid in their corner store they let
him have as many sour pickles
as his heart desired.
When his mother started her
long death it began with a fall,
the rose bushes catching her
leg and snapping the thin
honeycombed hip. Days before
she was found she had a chance
to grieve: no more boiled jellies
in the kitchen, no more
starching and folding. Her body recognized
it, all her fluids evaporated
into the sky.
Now, he is drowning.
Pneumonia floods the waterline
in his chest. As a child, his father hired
the best doctors to save him, when he
made a first false journey.
Then, the fevers held him up
against the bed sheets.
He notices a sour taste in his mouth,
coughs slightly.
The suction on the wall hisses
and he feels his cells drawn into it.
This time will be easier:
like flowers feeding their driest parts
then falling, full blown
over the table's edge.

NURSING INTERNSHIP, LA COUNTY, 1990

As the cancer patients died you smoked
another cigarette down by the dormitory pool, arm
dangling in the airless heat. A big
pink swimsuit wrapped you like a blanket.
We'd wrestled the pool from the medical students
for the afternoon, as they studied up on bones.

I was swaddling newborns all summer,
purple heads aiming for the room air. Their
bewildered mothers cradled them, fingers starred
in green tattoos, while palm trees waved
a first hello. It's a rough life:
the scratch of bad guitars outside the
Chicken Hut, girls trying on sunglasses so the men
can't see their eyes. Often it's a candle or a prayer between
themselves and death: a glance, a finger sign.

You fed the public hospital patients through various tubes
and afterwards drank private drinks down by the beach.
"It always starts so small" you say
gesturing at the loss of whole limbs and breasts,
the smallness of their cancer growing. Released
from work, I see the babies nightly in my dreams.
They rock themselves in plastic Bassinets.
Reach up with toes and fingers wiggling,
proud of all their parts.

ANOTHER LA POEM
(For Nurse Beverley)

I lay on the lumpy beach
in my striped bikini. You had decided
to show me Venice, with its fire walkers
and jugglers. We brought crackers
and sardines for a picnic, their
tiny bones snapped in my teeth. You
talked to me about world religion, and washing
the babies' heads. "I like to give them
their first baths" you said, liking it
that you could send them clean
into the world. You always remembered
to give the mothers sandwiches
after they delivered, reminded me
what work it was.
The waves went in and out, and people rubbed
themselves into the white beach.
I was trying to be a new nurse, and searching
for all their flaws.
Years later,
I think of you
when I smell that pink particular soap.
Holding my hands as if in prayer
under the warm faucet.

TRIP TO ALBUQUERQUE

The cultural advantage of pumping my own gas
makes my hand cramp up. Outside, the winds are pushing
wads of dust in steady piles. When I said I'd drive
alone, I found out what it means:
a large expensive car without the smell
of anyone's familiar sweat.

Sixteen upcoming exits lead to Albuquerque
what the West had won, then doubted.
People came to find the blankness,
then strung their lonesome lights and bottles in the dust.
I aim to where I think I might be going.
A trailer forms a village,
the prison makes a town.

Buying stamps and water for survival,
the radio tells of murder further south:
someone stuck a broom handle
through someone else's gut.
Another escapes jail by coating his skin
with Vaseline.
I picture sweat, thick and beady
sneaking down thin arms through glistening grease.

Back in Santa Fe, the tourists hang
like strung up peppers across verandahs.
Newly bought fetishes of animals
and teeth, ornament their limbs.
When the radio plays music, Indian chants
alternate with Latin salsa.
I drive towards Albuquerque, find a gas station
to check the water. Open the manual
to locate where the hood releases.

Every sense of ownership I feel
is not my own.

EEL

Elder faced,
old man whiskers
you shimmer the glass
slip yourself between the covers
of kelp. Tail and head synonymous,
your skin as slick as hair greased flat
for holiday—
you are what you are not:
no pelvic fins, no feelers,
footless. Not snake.
Not wallet, nor belt.
Not snail.
You'll never shimmy
through eel grass, too shallow.
Leaf vein bones
shore up your skin.
Thick centered, middle aged
you know the tight corners,
red rocks and half lit afternoons.
The air before the twister
strikes is like you:
green, pendulous vapor.
A storm crosses your one
large lip,
all teeth erupt
your body flicks a series of S's.
Cousin of the electric
your fatality is in the glance
alone,
a slippery, wet longing.

Christy Hurt

ON A PAINTING AT THE CHILDREN'S PSYCHIATRIC FACILITY

The moon was a huge, orange winter squash
that the child said he wouldn't eat. Refused.
He would and could
play with it instead and
in that mind, had thrown it
up in the right hand corner.
It landed high and deep
in crayola midnight blue,
with gray finger-streak clouds
dragging across its lumpy body.
It was no smooth moon.
A stick man waited on the silver hill,
and said "Me."
"Me" had the company of a stick tree
because the hill was much too lonely
a place to be. And besides,
a whisper, hissing sideways
through the branches, said
"I don't trust Me to be alone."
The throbbing orange moon was patient
with the scene. It had
all the time in the world.
Its orangeness kindled the sky
over a wide, turquoise meadow,
a slick dead-man's land from where
the stick man had walked and
from where the moon had risen,
budding and sobbing
with its awful pain and awful hope.

On the bottom of the painting, a note
to that singular person
who was Kindness:
   You are sososo nice to me
   and you are loving. I did not know
   me but now I do. Thank you.

ON THE SANDY RIVER, I FIND IN WOOD, THOUGHTS OF A BITTER SISTER

your curved body, sister, a casualty,
resting in a bank of dry grass.

it was you i saw
in a twist of blackened wood,
gnarled and scorched, dead-cold,
a still-insolent piece tossed, lost
from a campfire.

no smoke rising,
your desire for breath dispossessed.
no smolder kindling a golden thread of fire,
your desire for controversy congealed into darkest ash.
you gazed upwards through
the scuttling dance of leaves as only
a determined, carved, muted mask.

only stainedness instead of nakedness.

yet?
yet with the sharp knowledge
your breasts were dark-edged knots
thrusting outward, bare challenges
for swimmers marching over you
to the river's wide greenness,
to a cool, long-lapping current
you would never reach,
so despise.

your sullen wood, at its thighs,
womanly split. but as a non-brilliant sister
no longer waiting. left. a wood
sooted, leaf-shadowed, sorrowed,
warring with neither hopes or dilemmas.

barren, tenacious sister,
set apart, resistant to rebounding,

to the redoubling sounds of love,
your wood forcefully silent and dark,
in all your sacrifices,
you were selfish,
you were constrained,
seared defiant, without bud or root.

sister, deaconess
of the bitter-boned, to see
what you see from where you lie.
the grass is high,
the leaves break the sky,
and your loveliness, burnt and aloof.

MY SISTER'S PHOTO . . . DATED 1973 . . . SHE'S TWENTY YEARS OLD AND VERY PRETTY

we searched for her, for her body
with a face which was
my sister's. seeking out a drowned body
that a swollen childish river wanted to
suck and hoard to itself,
a shameful treasure stuffed
under a log jam.

   i remember she was raped real young.

for a breach of days and nights,
we took to hoping, angling
with gigantic hooks, hoping to
salvage her body from the river's
slag. we crawled waist-high into turbulence,
we were nearly gulped and swallowed.
mad, we sunk our hate into the muck and
chain-sawed through wood and water,
grappled, wondered
if the river had left her
whole or gashed.

   i remember she became a prostitute.

unshaven, sleepless, groping—
we said we would not go home
until we found her. we felt selfish.
our eyes and bones ran cold with
the thought of her—her legs, shoulders,
loins, ribs, kidneys, brains, her heart—
swimming loose, becoming
the river. when the river flung
itself into our gaping mouths,
we tasted her.

*i remember she disappeared
when i was thirteen and
that i loved her and wanted her home.*

*(written after a week of watching rory on the evening news...
searching for his sister's body in the toutle river...may 3, 1997)*

Sabine Miller

HEADACHE ROCK

The girls ask if I am praying.
He's tied my tongue in knots
and I am not praying nor dying

I husband the air I breathe
like others ration water.
There is sun on the flat parts,

the wrinkles on the dimes
I give them for rock candy.

The problem with spring is·
I can't close my eyes on it

I want to be free of desire.
Tomorrow they'll call me
Headache Rock.

Ursula Irwin

BRUSH STROKES

    If I had not
kept the feather
  of the yellow chickadee,

    if I had not
  taped it into my notebook,
I would have

    forgotten that Sunday morning,
 the snow and the feathers
of the chickadee lying
      like Chinese brush strokes
  on the immaculate canvas.

        Small
lovely, like fine combs. No bones. Charcoal gray
      tipped,
  charcoal gray spined, and yellow.
  And sleek, and two

down feathers that kept
  the blood warm.

BENEDICTION

There had been drifted commitments,
shifting alliances of grass and leaves
and junipers.

Now the garden lets the gardener find
its lines:

the terraced field stones,
a hole below one large stone, perhaps
for a burrowing animal or the snake
I saw here two summers ago, swishing
through soft grass.

   It drew its own lines.
      I never knew where.

The lines he uncovers all faded
for her, the plumber's wife.

She lost her boundaries and the garden grew
crazy. She kept a duck in the basement,
looked for trails of slugs, turning
stones, prying off
the wet, soft bodies. She hung her laundry
in the neighbor's yard, then
wandered in her nightgown
into the forest, every turn
another step toward a perfection only she
understood.

The gardener found what she lost:
that ring around the apple tree,
bump-outs of relief
from the rectangular property, a lovely
curve of bluebells under the spiraea that dismisses
the corner.

Under the blooming laurel—
look at that benediction of lilies
of the valley over the space they now possess—
like the pastor sending off the
Sunday congregation, opening green hands
"May the blessing of the Lord
be with you."

   I like to follow their lines
  finish
the curved motion whose end I cannot see.
   intrigued to complete it, lose myself

in her recovered
  faded rose, white, indigo,
cerulean blue.

Trudy Godat

TREED

At twenty-three he is
a colorful man with a checkered future,

as generations fall from him.
We will never know

any of them—he doesn't either.
Exactly how many?

A torrential rainstorm
he floods our living.

I iron our clothes
to keep things straight, tidy.

When others drift
off to sleep, we all, placed

like barbies in a doll house, lie stiff
for him to pick the house

up and shake it. (In a dream;
I was in a tree placing secrets
in the bark.) Each night I bundle the knives
in cloth and hide them under my mattress.

As a lazy sun just nudges
the horizon the waiting

is over. His irreverent spit
lands on the crucifix. Scooping it

from the wall I lay it with the already bundled
knives. I wonder if the bark can hold. I hear

from my bedroom
it has begun.

UNTITLED
(For my mother and her mother)

It is how she rolls.
From the center
Outward. A fresh mound
And then works
It into a large circle
Until the thinness allows no more
Rolling. Edges tattered
And only barely
There. This is her achievement.

ENCLOSING THE CIRCLE

Each time
I try to rescue her memories,
as they seep from their container.

This time
Ten feet before I reach her,
I stop and watch, hoping to capture a hint
of one of her years already history.

Her meager body poured into a chair,
Her innards have no privacy.
Each joint, bone and deformity visible
through flesh
          wants out.

Can regression return her to
the fluid of the womb?

I can't ignore
her fresh, Soft Ginger lipstick
gently disregarding the lines of her mouth.

I wander after her wandering mind,
and try to remember where I've been.

Finally, I kneel beside her chair.
Yellowing around the edges of the whites,
her eyes strain upward to encounter mine.

As if a transfusion has taken place,
between us, her cheeks fill with blood
as mine drain slightly.

SCATTERED OUT

Many to follow. Like the veins
in my mother's legs.

I picked the small gray one. It pulled me
away from the ocean and led up

the side of a minor mountain. The car open
like a rolled back can of sardines.
White, quick, rented. I drove through

the blue-orange afternoon splitting it.
Then left it trailing as I moved through

the air into the black starlessness. Winding sharper
I drove faster with each corner.

On my ascent the road narrowed as canyons deepened
on either side. High fences grew higher.

Atop, high beams cut in and targeted
a baby deer. I shut down

everything and froze in the middle
of the road. If he could bound the fence

from his fear I wanted to miss the view.

Carl Adamshick

SENSE
(After Eavan Boland)

This is where the sweet onion is cut
and the oil with arugula, shaped

by a handsome bottle,
is concerned with a blue plate

of kalamatas.
Bread brushed with red wine.

A rosewood table set
in still life. Blood

oranges and silver lighted
by an eclipsed afternoon. Cracked

pomegranates, their fish eggs
loose. The moment

turns inward, assembling.
Birth. Scents of rosemary

and the tiny flowers of thyme.
The becoming shifts

closer. All the gatherings
arrive. The summation,

a snifter of bloomed saffron,
a new angle of perception.

LIZBETH

lizbeth likes to drink black tea.
she loves the ephemera:
spoons, cups, steeping pots.
she takes her glasses off, scrunches
up on the couch.
lizbeth loves the idea of reading
more than the act itself.

regret is supposed to happen after years of denial.

lizbeth never messes with her hair
or clothes or family matters.
she likes coltrane
in the mornings,
parker after dinner, sometimes
lizbeth just sits on her bed
before getting under the covers.

apologies aren't worth much after awhile.

when lizbeth was young
she wanted boys
to touch her, she loved
moccasins, the black that fell
from fireworks, and hummingbirds.
lizbeth still dreams
and allows men to touch her.

dignity is so small sometimes, so small.

lizbeth loves the tiny rituals
of bathtaking;
the waver of candlelight.
she can cover an emotion
to where the inattentive
never notice. lizbeth finds herself
in reflection then loses focus.

platitudes during difficulties never help.

lizbeth at the greenhouse
deliberate with flowers.
she wipes her hands on her pants
and all concerns
leave her. she moves
powerful, an ocean, a bell,
her search for balance gathers here.

oh lizbeth you should see how the center is held.

WORSHIP

I'm thinking of you right now.
   I'm smelling my hands and thinking
of the naked slopes of your shoulders,
    straining neck muscles, ear.
Afternoons I might
   cater to your whims,
         the flick of your wrist,
feel something other than the vacuous light

   of what I am.

Tell me stories of lineage,

       how you move from day to day,

   reasons knowledge is uncertain,
              reason to me.

I'll fix you jasmine tea
   the way you like it,
       a spoon and a half of sugar,
          a good cloud of cream.
   I'll bring raspberries and kumquats
and place the cold fruit-gems
       in your mouth
one by one.

Empty the world

   of all meaning,

of everything

   except this.

Touch.

—CUSTOMS OF GRACE

There is morel and respect,
sweet basil and fennel tranquil before death,
the lenitive pond and linden
in gentle fall light;
habit is to give and be given.

Michele Glazer

LETTER

   How are you? I hate to ask. I got your nails.
The old man at Winks who couldn't find them found them
on a back shelf. He called them *infinitesimal*.
They are for someone I said who mounts endangered
butterflies on velvet-covered coreboard
because he wants something beautiful that won't get away
                                              against a backdrop
that will keep him from valuing the whole thing over much.
Then I had another thought. I didn't write it down and I lost it.
That's the way I am now.
What is the social context of cells?

   Today it snowed so I read about the bower bird though cause
and effect is mostly tenuous like today and yesterday
but get this, the bower bird picks blue
to make its nest. Blue this, blue that.
The object attends but, really,
weather's what's interesting.
Everytime it just sits down to what it is.
When the call came to come in, talk in person
it must have added up. That mock-bronchial cough.
The day's terminal
appointment   shit
I almost envy you almost
knowing where you
locate the infinite.   Sick!
I'm afraid of what you'll miss John.
Of missing you. Today Jeff said of a moment
in a poem I wrote, "I hate those canned moments in second
                                      person direct address
when the reader knows it's him who is really being addressed.
                                                    Romantic!"
Does your life feel different, the way immediately you know
when the tunnel is no longer France, it has become Italy?
That darkness isn't the same and the train rumbles
the tracks with a different racket. What I can't ask you
couldn't tell me. The darkness

is the same. Write soon. Forgive me
when I use you.
Holding his cup of mucous, cells, erratica, pus, what else?
Then something-other's clumsy-handed someone and it spills.

ALL THAT IN THE VOICE I HAVE ADOPTED FOR THIS LIE

(For J. K.)

Fresh figs blacken and sweeten.
The Mediterranean sun lengthens and roots,
tipped by a nimble surer than a dowser's wand, sink
like the dream into the dreamer.
On top a woman walks about.
To wend the invisible is to know
the obstacle before they meet.
She knows these leaves
are fleshy with an inference
she restrains herself from touching and feels lush
in her restraint.
Too-sweet, the figs
rot.

   She's had enough, she knows what they are doing,
roots waking to receding water.
Naked, in the shower, and her feet, naked too, of course, she
                                                                                              stands
inches deep in the brackish back-up, the color swirling   —no
no-color—   it's the shadow
cast by water,
an appalling and miraculous
root-soup.

   They are waking and she knows it.
There is no wobble down there.
All direction is toward desire
if desire's felt. How often she is
two ways at once.
She is old and bends
easily. She is thin.
She is on her knees, with both hands
she wends the snake down in.

SCIENCE

Larkspur——bluemoss——his deciduous hands——
oh, but why would you want to?
He is somber honey.
He is a mouthful of bees.

Tom Richards

LESSONS OF A BLACKSMITH

If a man could be
perfect his hands
would tell me.
Yours a tome
I could not read.
When the perfect house burnt
you built another,
better.
You were the ink
in Hemingway's pen.
Salt and a white
cotton tank-top
cling to a man's body.
Arms built between
anvil and hammer
carry buckets of large
blue berries
the size of my eyes.
Grandfather
were you perfect?
Are my tears
the memories
of your sweat?
My emotions
the history
of your muscles?
Singing coins flew
from your long fingers,
sparks from an anvil,
silver in the grass.
I searched and found
decoys.
I gleaned nothing!
I know none of your stories.
None were told.
I am listening
to your movements

with my memory
and wondering—
what did you tell me
when you said nothing?

WITH HER HUSBAND...

in the next room,
she asked you,
Do you believe in picnics?
Yes, you said, I do

believe in picnics.
Then dreaming your dream,
she left her husband.
In this dream you and her

lying on your stomachs
atop a thickquilt of moss
reading books, whose pages
became white

doves, by firelight in a home,
with no ceiling or walls,
floating in a care less darkness
with sparking embers as stars.

In this dream
her fingers woven with yours,
palms pressed like naked bellies,
as you walked

down a crowded street where people
could see two lovers walking.
Asphalt became sand,
and the white

doves became sea gulls
selling, in screams,
the ocean. The sand
at your feet was a con-

duit for warmth. The waves
placed a lace ribbon of foam
at your feet. In it—perfect
letters, forming perfect words.

Again: Do you believe
in picnics? Yes, you said,
would you like to come to mine?
Palimpsest waves come in

and out, over the unsaid sand.
Palimpsest letters pushed in
pulled out, over the unsaid sand.
The tide is the ocean

pulled by the moon.
No! You screamed
softly. This is not a picnic,
only me praising the waves. You

belong to the moon.
—These words
scripted for you
by the waves themselves.

Sometimes the moon's pull is strong,
beach becomes desert. You would not
doubt the return. You stood by a cactus
and waited for the waves, while screaming

gulls became quiescent vultures.
You spread your blanket and opened
the wine. As you waited for the waves
already the ants began to gather.

FIVE A.M. IN THE JERICHO BEACH HOSTEL

Teen angst paraded about
like mad ants stirred
by hormonal sticks.
I slept on the lobby
couch 'til eight,
moved from my plastic bed
by an English mustache,
snoring potatoes,
in bunk-28 below me.
During the second night,
in a new room,
I was accompanied
by a quartet of human throats:
a boat gnawing at a dock,
a dresser pulled across the floor
of a ceiling, a needle repeatedly
circling the end
of a record, and the muffled
voice of a child
in an unknown room.
I took to the lobby,
but chased by the electric sucking
of Canadian repressions
and cleanliness I sunk to the cool
of the TV room where I rested
in episodic dream channels
soon awoken by ants.
There was that,
and the fact of the diminished
sense of humor of their police,
now mounted in Chryslers,
that brought me back home
two days ahead of schedule.

Arthur Irwin

SEAGULLS

Gulls, with their fragile structed
wings, with their piercing mannequin
sight, hover above
fish-kidney docks
the apex of the food chain
the lords of fisheads, guts & skin
(with a special fondness for eyes).

They ever follow the fishing fleets
wheeling on kite wings
born by the updrafts
of a rising isotherm, in a skelter
carousel. How do they know—
these hawks of refuse—
when bait will be chummed,
when chopped herring and squid
will enter the wake,
causing a bubbling of fins
and a ravenous squawking from above.
Diving, they scoop the salty brine.

And once more ashore
they sit like little Solomons
on corrugated roof-ridges
scanning the possibilities—the absolute
potential for a snack—to be
cornered with outstretched wing
and talon—to be torn, if need
be, from the beaks of
companionable gourmets.

In the evenings the sea-breezes
rise, balancing the warmth of the land,
flowing salt in faint wafts
to moisture-starved souls.
And the gulls rise in stratified
flocks—a thousand drunkards' paths.

Kelly Lenox Allan

MEMORIES LIKE THIS

Flying fish caught
in the sun: each sharp scale.
After dark, fireflies in the loose air
under trees; in a jar breathing
through chiseled holes. At every
heel-strike the sparking of scuffed sand.

I dig my toes among fibers of crabgrass,
pry for a grip into scaly bark—the old pine,
its needles dark against a negative sky;
sulfur on the wind.

Their sound lost in distance, fireworks burst
and fall, purple and green, like the blown seed
of dandelion. It is only night.

This purl into new skin like wool
heathered with plankton, insects, fire.

DOWSING

I leave Arizona arid—the mustard burns
and the price of water is too high.

To bisect is human so I lay down dusty tracks all the way
to Minnesota. At the filling station a dry man stutters
that I must turn right—I have no boat, he tells me,
and already, the water is too high:

sharp-angled shoals of rooftops, reefs
of fence and dike. Turning right, then, I venture into
                                              a cheese
of potholes. Even here, the water is getting too high.

I experience Duluth, Sault Ste. Marie: logical events
in a periodic landscape without mowers.
The Red's flood won't find Lake Superior: the sound
of motor boats and helicopters will ride
the river-water north, dropping high into Canada;

Time is perched between these inland seas, one
reincarnate. Blades of grass replay their one riff.
I quiet my browning foliage. Coach brings the sophomores
out for a cross-country run. The pack stops
at a footbridge—already, the water is too high.

The story of this bisect: one half and its ocean
on one side; on the other, the other and its.
In between is everything. I drive, not letting
time get too far behind. Before two oceans, I'll cross
two high snows, rushing, already, into water.

A DRIVER. A HEART ATTACK.

At his memorial service I spill
A pitcher of hot tea all over the drink table;
Stain my clothes, the napkins, the floor.
The clean spoons sparkle.

Our collective smile is missing a front tooth.

This afternoon the clouds kept
All the beams but one: *the sun*
Still shines above these sleet-nests.
As their roiling underbelly disperses
We uncover our heads, walk erect,
Lay eyes on each horizon.

THIS SEASON

Needle-sharp screeching
rains through my eyes, skewed

                                        Dim days
                                        it's just hard

Cubist colors jostle for spots
on their wheel; too soon it spins

                                        To stand, to walk. I'm tired
                                        of sleep. Why are days?

With a discordant whine like my
old blow-dryer, like the tree-chippers

                                        My home is a framework
                                                    of chores
                                        bound together by plaster,
                                                    by some paint.

Hauled by goldfish-colored trucks
to untangle a wet gale's mauling.

                                        I leave the lights on all
                                                    day because
                                        it doesn't seem like it, not
                                            because I'm going
                                                      anywhere.

The guy in the cherry picker revs his chainsaw,
rips through knots of limb and wire.

                                        Sometimes I forget and
                                                       wander
                                        through these rooms like
                                               in that dream
                                        where I can't keep my eyes
                                                          open.

Trunk and bark—their stores of sunlight—fracture
into severed rainbows falling
through whirling blades.

                                        Where is the light

Quiet?

Eric Hull

UNTITLED

I thought of you tonight
as I sat down on the toilet,
as I often do—
think of you,
not sit on the toilet.
That too,
but think of you
mostly
I do
nowhere near the toilet!
But tonight
I thought of you on the toilet—
tonight, while on the toilet,
I thought of you
and romance vanished.
This is me, I thought.
This is who I long for her to love.

UNTITLED

I drove by the tree
you stood under
I think
I am happy to say
I wasn't
sure which tree
you stood under
in the spring
and lifted
your face to feel
damp pink petals fall
onto your face and hair
and stay
I said
it is hard not to love you
when you do things like that
and you
said you were
sorry

THE PATCH

There on his knees,
his bald head flushed from brow
to hairline, spotted
with sweat
like when he ate Mexican food,
was my father. My room smelled of

adhesive.
Try to find the patch.
The what?
The patch in the carpet!
I looked in the doorway
between my room and his.

I failed.
Would he have asked me to find it
if it could possibly be found?
I only
wanted my room back.
He did it for me, I know—

the new paneling.
This silence milled
the trim himself
because he had a hard time
saying, to his son
who cried too easily and hit

the other team too softly, but
mostly just held on
until someone
bigger,
bolder came
along to finish the job,

I love you.
It was not what I wanted,

but now I can say it was kind
at the time
it was ancient
books in a very tight tongue

behind
a locked door
smelling. Now
I say it is enough—
I read the books
in his firm handshake

and his *Could you
help me move the porch swing
into the basement?*
Now the door is open.
The room is lit
with a 67 year old dawn.

Mary Misel

GRINDING

I take it to the grinding wheel,
Sparks fly as pieces of odd metal liberate themselves.
My eyes try to close behind the rain of sparks,
Scratching at the plastic shield, trying to get in.
I'm making it fit, making it of use.
Moving the steel continuously across the stone,
Avoiding the pitting of the stone, keeping it smooth
                                              and rounded.
Even wear is all we ever want from a stone
Destroying itself to make things useful. Even wear.

Pieces of slag that buried my steel
Throw themselves, on fire,
Through our atmosphere.
The air tastes of steel, burn and smolder,
Heat deep, from friction gives the steel
More hardness, and the hands avoid
But always touch, by accident leaving mark of steel
On body, steel marked by body, scars shared.

Slag perches everywhere, in windowsills, under furniture,
No containing it, it lives on brooms never finding it all.
Steel, worked and polished to fit,
Perfectly, proudly, prices are paid.
The useless leaving behind
The useful and moving on.

Michael Griggs

LETTER TO A CRUEL MOTHER
(Suprasyl, January 1997)

Poland, you mother
land of liberty,
you insist on making
promises you cannot keep.

Your land used up, your people used up,
your shit brown air—no day or night,
or light to tell the difference by.
Your monuments to death, death, death
ground underfoot by generations
of the fearful, the overgrown depositories
of mortality, newly pregnant with frights
aspiring to crawl from your womb.

And now the new death moves crablike,
sideways across the cities,
pinching out your children's life
with its Burger Kings and Pizza Huts.
But you are silent and unrepentant,
because you suckled kings,
and balanced peasant huts upon your hips.
It's all the same to you.

I keep myself from you.
I will not call you weekends
or say those words you use
to shame the guilty, false response.
I will visit, and be polite,
and talk of unimportant things,
but I will not acknowledge
from where I come.

Outside the window,
newly whitened birch and pine are telling me
it's time I held you in my arms.

Patricia Staton Thomas

HEX, UNHEX

Espressoed, I'm up for the stellar
roofer to come and stop the leaks.
I know it'll take a spell.

But see for yourself. Time and rain—
only a few stains mark the loss
inside. If I can wait fast

enough, cross my fingers, kiss a frog,
maybe we can go back
and just patch it.

Yesterday, the wizard of loose floorboards,
looking down,
found tenants—a rotting footing,

post and block "riddled with bugs."
That's life. Tiny Al Capones
Gatling holes in our cedar.

We settle in the sand.
Every ten years or so, he said,
we should have shored it up.

Wonderful. Having no wand,
we looked away. Jimmy Stewart
and Donna Reed

never had to call the exterminator.
Is it a sign the chimney angel
won't return my calls?

Upstairs I'll chip
the powdering plaster from the bricks
to weigh the damage—

story has it the old chimneys

are mortared with everyday beach sand.
Unsticking,

it wants to shift for itself.
It's lost its charm.
Let it go? If I went, I'd go,

I would not curse what was alchemy.

FATHER'S DAY AT SNAPP'S COTTAGES

When the smallest boy steps up to the plate,
under a sky that stone color of blue,
the field grows inward, rounds down
to the size of a small yard.
The child swings and swings
without fear. A hawk veers in the infinite blue.

Iron filings toward a magnet—
the families file in
across the hill of mowed dandelions.
How they—we—are lured by his diminutive size,
the pull of his unknowing
swinging a wide arc around him.

He draws us in.
Geometry in his pocket,
he turns a diamond into a ring.

POMMES DE TERRE

The man roasting in a dark suit under the leaves of my holly tree
begs my pardon with a scrubbed and starched child.
His paper leaflets curl and grow old in the light.
Next to my hill of potatoes, this child amounts to
barely anything. Neither fruit nor root,
she is clearly not his offspring—clearly an exotic species
sprouting from less flinty soil. He extends

Tidings.
I am sorry. I am up to here in my potatoes. I am certain
this is for a good cause, Sunday and all, and I think
if I were as charitable as you I would look up and be glad
for your expectations. Later, I will wash my hands of them.
No matter, my hands are already so dirty
the dark type on those pages won't rub off.

The girl is another matter. I will blame you
for this pale, leggy spud, planting her white
patent leather shoes in my precious pommes de terre.
Somebody's love apple.
Somebody's potassium and phosphorous, somebody's runners
outside your will, outside mine,
finding their way through the darkness.

MALADIES OF THE HEART, VOL. 7

Through a quadrant-shaped window
the odd fauna,
or is it flora
that is the heart. Your heart
on screen is liquid,
is semi-solid, anatomic,
undulating inside the body's closed ocean.

Ectopics
was spoken by the doctor,
and *bundle branch block*,
days ago.

In ultra-
sound it's a black, jumbled muscle,
devoid of any visible branchings,
any breathing
tubes, to the surface,
quivering,
pulsing in its brine a-
rhythmically,
as if less
familiar with its role as keeper of the
time
than one would hope.

The black sea
anemone
blossoming near the top
of the heart, your heart,
the ivory fingered-technician says is blood,
pooling.
Electrical, I am learning,
it has to find its own way
around the
block, he says, firing off bursts
of red and blue, animating the screen

with the squid-like explosions
of an old Jules Verne movie.
The blue marks the blood en-
tering, exiting is the red,
the real-life-and-death heart-to-body
sonar.
In a few days
a city cardiologist will view
the video. Regardless of us,
screen and technician linger on
Tricuspid Valve,
imprinted there in passionless,
flat script. Live,
his voice says,
the technology shows no damage.

Your live heart
on hold in this
interval,
laid open between glass and ground,
logged-in on film and syn-
thesized sound—
*de whew wup, de whew wup, de
wh...wu-wuhp,* a
music for sturgeon and other bottom fish—
choreographing its own
submarine waltz,
the dips and sways, the truth
of its hesitation
making up for the hold
with a two-step, an old step
I know you know,
we both know—
the one when we dance our dance
I never can follow. The one with the edge
I never can follow you over.

LOVE POEM

I will steal every fish you give me.
With my tongue I will skim every gifted carcass.
I will steal the very hearts I cut from trout
and make them into valentines. The scissors will cut my hands
I will hunker down and crawl inside you.
If I were a swan I wouldn't know how to wrinkle or weep.
If I were a swan I wouldn't know how to sweat.
If I were a swan I wouldn't have settled in so close
you could hear my river, wouldn't have let you shine
your face with the oil pressed from my feathers,
hone your teeth on my raw voice edges,
or squeeze the air from my still-heaving lungs.
Such caresses might be punishment enough,
if enough were enough.
I will forget where I left my fish, my ocean, my gravel,
my leeches and rock salt, my grandfather's hymns.
And when the air is still,
when I fall into bed
I am surrounded,
and none of them strangers.

THE WRITERS COLLECTIVE:

CARL ADAMSHICK was born tall in the midwest. He read his first book when he was 21, has slowly turned to language, to poetry, for long tall, skinny words.

KELLY LENOX ALLAN was born near Princeton, New Jersey. Her itinerant life, begun when she was two weeks old, came to a halt in 1989 when she moved to Portland where she lives with her husband, two sons and their gerbil. She leads poetry workshops for elementary students in a Portland public school and is an associate editor of *Rain City Review*. Her poems have appeared in *Poet Lore, Word Wrights!,* and *Poetry Motel*.

SOPHIE CRAWFORD lives with her cat, an indomitable tabby, in S.E. Portland. In 1990 she received an MFA in Creative Writing from the University of Oregon. Her poems have appeared in various journals including *Puerto del Sol, Mississippi Valley Review, Fireweed,* and *Rain City Review*. She is working on a book-length collection of her poems.

MICHELE GLAZER's book, *It Is Hard to Look At What We Came to Think We'd Come to See*, was published in late 1997 by the University of Pittsburgh Press. She has received fellowships from Oregon Literary Arts, the University of Iowa, and the National Endowment for the Arts. She works for the Nature Conservancy.

TRUDY GODAT was born and raised in rural Oregon. She graduated from the school of hard knocks, then graduated *summa cum laude* from Portland State University with a B.S. in psychology. She loves her nieces and nephews without limit and will understand when they are in transition, as she is now.

MELANIE GREEN's various careers have included motorcycle salesperson, ski instructor, and daycare supervisor. Currently she is a nature photographer and races motorcycles, jet skis, and helicopters at local video arcades.

MICHAEL GRIGGS has been working in the theater for the past twenty-nine years as a director, actor, administrator, presenter, and educator. He is the former Artistic Director of The New Rose Theatre in Portland, Oregon (1985-89), and Bear Republic Theater of Santa Cruz, California (1974-85), and currently serves as Artistic Director of the Portland International Performance Festival, which he founded in 1991. His local directing credits include Artists Repertory Theatre, Storefront Theatre, and Interstate Firehouse Cultural Center. He has directed more than 75 productions in regional professional and educational theatre, and is an adjunct faculty member in theater at Portland State University and Linfield College. He recently returned from directing his own adaptations of *The Dybbuk* in Budapest, Hungary with R.S.9, and in Bialystok, Poland with Wierszalin, in 1996-97.

ERIC HULL is a writer and actor living in Portland. A native of the Rose City, he enjoys gardening and Argentine Tango.

CHRISTY HURT was born in Denver, Colorado under a bad sign: "NOW HIRING GRAPEFRUIT 6/$1" and hence developed at an early age an interest in the peculiar, especially when it comes to "dysfunctional" family, or, people in general. Consequently, she began writing under the cover of the small ironies of life a couple of years ago.

ARTHUR IRWIN lives in Portland, Oregon.

URSULA IRWIN teaches English at Mt. Hood Community College and lives in Portland, Oregon.

TRACY KLEIN was born and remains in Portland, Oregon. She took a brief detour during nursing school to Los Angeles, which inspired a few of these poems. A nurse practitioner by trade, she has read for the Portland Poetry Festival, Artquake, and the Mountain Writers Series.

KATHARINE MILLER, a native New Yorker, moved to Portland in 1992. She has been a member of the Writers Collective since 1993. Known as Kate, she works as a librarian in Tigard, Oregon. Kate and her husband live with their ferocious cat on the east bank of the Willamette River.

SABINE MILLER was born in Seattle, raised in Miami and schooled in Montreal and Portland. She now lives in California where she writes poetry and observes slug behavior.

MARY MISEL lives in Gaston, Oregon

QUIGLEY PROVOST-LANDRUM is a native Texan transplanted to the Pacific Northwest from Austin. She currently resides in Portland, Oregon with her ornery husband and
their two cats, Juno and Ludwig.

TOM RICHARDS writes in Portland, Oregon, where he has lived since 1982.

RICHARD SANDERS is a Portland writer and teacher.

PATRICIA STATON THOMAS worked as an advertising copywriter, a hardware store clerk, and a radio host before she and her husband started a business making miniature houses for collectors. She has published a number of poems and in 1995 received an Artist Trust Fellowship in Literature, funded by the Washington State Arts Commission and the NEA. She has a play in the works called "Life with the Dead Man," and lives in the rainiest county in the continental United States.